I'm Moving Again...

Gretchen Flicker
1812 Overland Avenue #304
Los Angeles, CA 90025

(310) 234-1256

As of April 1, 1998

I HATE Men
225 Reasons Why You Should, Too

Crane Hill
PUBLISHERS
BIRMINGHAM, ALABAMA
1997

I HATE Men
225 Reasons Why You Should, Too

by Susan Murphy

CRANE HILL
PUBLISHERS

Copyright 1997 by Susan Murphy

All rights reserved
Printed in the United States of America
Published by Crane Hill Publishers
Library of Congress Cataloging-in-Publication Data

Murphy, Susan, 1954-
  I hate men : 225 reasons why you should, too / by Susan Murphy.
    p.   cm.
  ISBN 1-57587-053-3
  1. Men — Humor. I. Title.
PN6231.M45I43   1997
818'.5402--dc21   96-53405
                                                                            CIP

10   9   8   7   6   5   4   3   2   1

I HATE MEN

Okay ... maybe "hate" is too strong a word. Let's just say there are certain testosterone-linked behaviors I find hard to understand. For instance ...

1. Men think there is a simple answer for everything.

I HATE MEN

2. Men are experts at appearing busy without actually being helpful.

3. Men would rather be torn apart by wild boars than talk about their feelings.

4. Men consider salsa a vegetable.

5. Men fall sleep whenever they are tired, even if you have company.

6. Men think asking for directions is the equivalent of castration.

7. Men see Home Depot as the temple of all that is hardware.

8. Men do all their heavy reading in the bathroom.

9. Men consider the ability to make rude body noises at will a genuine talent.

10. Men take up the whole couch, get a death grip on the remote control, turn on any cable-access sporting event, and then fall asleep 15 minutes into the game.

11. If you turn off the TV, men wake up immediately and say, "I was watching that!"

12. Men never smell messy diapers.

13. Every man wishes his wife were more like his mother.

14. Every man wishes his wife were more like his dog.

15. Men like to be needed ... except during the ball game.

16. Men just don't get *Bridges of Madison County.*

17. Men consider beer the perfect food.

18. Men practice deficit dieting, as in "At least I didn't have two scoops of ice cream on my pie."

19. Every man thinks there's really not that much difference between him and Steven Seagal.

20. Men think John Wayne should be canonized.

21. Men have selective hearing: They can tell if the car's fan belt is loose but can not hear "Please take out the trash."

22. Men have selective memory: They can quote the ERA of any baseball player but forget your anniversary.

23. Men consider 2-liter bottles single-serving containers.

24. Men eat Spam.

25. Men scream at the referees on TV.

26. Men think jalapenos are not really good unless they make you sweat.

27. Men don't know *Baywatch* is a show about lifeguards.

28. Men think checkbooks are for wimps.

29. Men use toothpicks.

30. Men insist that cars be spotless but have no problem with mold growing on shower curtains.

31. When men offer to bring something to a party, it's a 6-pack of beer, which they drink themselves.

32. Men snore loud enough to wake themselves up ... and everyone else within a 5-mile radius.

33. Men smell a shirt before they wear it.

34. If a shirt does not pass the smell test, men spray it with Lysol and throw it into the dryer.

35. Men eat pork rinds and Cornuts.

36. Men spit.

37. Before embarking on any type of sporting activity, men must buy $150 of professional-quality equipment.

38. Men will sit and watch a football game between ... well, it really doesn't matter.

39. Men believe their favorite team would be winning today if they were the coach.

40. Men don't change toilet paper rolls.

41. Men don't understand: coasters.

42. ... shelf paper.

43. ... Hallmark stores.

44. ... gossip.

45. ... scented candles, scented soap, scented anything except car air fresheners.

46. Men think they have a better system for everything.

47. Men will click past a presidential press conference, Mother Teresa addressing the U.N., and a special about possible life on Mars to watch *Shade Tree Mechanic.*

48. Men think wrapping a gift is a waste of time.

49. Men think "I guess so" is an apology.

50. Men buy new underwear rather than run a load of wash.

51. Men pack for a week's vacation in a duffel bag.

52. Men refuse to check their luggage, and they insist that their golf clubs will indeed fit in the overhead bin.

53. Men call 18 holes of golf a business outing.

54. When men watch the children, they call it baby-sitting.

55. When men do housework, they are "helping you."

56. Men make an announcement whenever they do anything that approaches being helpful, as in "I just rinsed out my glass."

57. Men think building a fire is like performing a Japanese tea ceremony.

58. Men help: get the kids ready for bed by tickling them until they wet their pajamas.

59. ... get ready for company by waxing the lawnmower.

60. ... dust by running their stocking feet over the coffee table.

61. ... get ready to leave on vacation by arranging their drill bits by size.

62. ... send Christmas cards by leaving the stack you wrote, stamped, and addressed on the seat of the car until January 6th.

63. No man likes to get a new wallet because he has to go to the trouble of molding it to his backside all over again.

64. Men have not changed their basic clothing style in centuries, except for that brief leisure suit/Nehru jacket episode, which they refuse to discuss.

65. Men don't understand why women don't want a Naugahyde recliner next to a Louis XIV armoire.

66. Men think bathroom telephones in hotels are a great idea.

67. Men think the perfect gift is whatever is closest to the cash register at Kmart.

68. Men will pay $5 to have a Daisy Seal-A-Meal wrapped.

69. Men punch holes in the bottom of chocolates to see what flavor they are.

70. Men think greeting cards are for wimps.

71. Men don't understand why anyone would pay more than $7 for a haircut.

72. Men relax by not showering or shaving.

73. Men stand in front of the mirror and say, "Yeah ... I've still got it."

74. Men think "love handles" is an affectionate term.

75. Men are always more tired than you are.

76. Men moan when they have a hangnail.

77. Men use crutches for a sprained toe.

78. Men will pay to: sit in a 50,000-seat auditorium and see fish weighed.

79. ... wear earplugs and watch a giant tractor shoot flames out of its tailpipe.

80. ... watch cars smash into each other until only one is left running.

81. ... see Michael Jordan do anything at all.

82. Men pledge organizations that have initiation rites of chugging a gallon of beer and allowing your brother members to beat you within an inch of your life.

83. Men put on fluorescent orange jumpsuits and sit in trees all day to fool deer.

84. Men fantasize about having a bar complete with a jukebox in the basement.

85. When a man wears a toupee, he doesn't think anyone knows it.

86. Men sit on the couch for 2 hours waiting for you to get up and then say, "While you're up ... "

87. Men think that if you pick up the remote control, you are invading their personal space.

88. Men will take a miniature TV to a football game so they can watch another game at the same time.

89. On long distance trips men stop only when THEY have to go to the bathroom.

90. Men take the kids trick-or-treating and steal their candy.

91. Men take the biggest portion from the serving platter even when you have dinner guests.

92. Men drink out of the milk carton.

93. Men think napkins are for wimps.

94. Men drink all but 2 ounces of juice and put the container back in the refrigerator.

95. Men never notice dog accidents.

96. Men do not answer the phone unless they think it's for them.

97. Men think "Why go out for a hamburger when you have steak at home?" is a compliment.

98. Men buy a car because it can go from 0 to 60 in 6 seconds even though they will only be driving it during rush hour traffic to and from work.

99. Men want a barber named Bob, not a hair stylist named Raul.

100. Men pop the hood of the car and look inside even though they have no earthly idea what to do once the hood is open.

101. Men think assembly instructions are for wimps.

102. Men pretend they know how to fix everything.

103. Men try to fix everything.

104. Men think you are betraying them when you call a repairman after they have tried to fix something.

105. When a man gets a new toy (a car, Weed Eater, whatever) you must repeatedly tell him how wonderful it is.

106. Men reward people they really care about by making rude noises in front of them and forgetting their birthdays.

107. Men think Christmas shopping before Christmas Eve is rushing the season.

108. Men have no idea what Santa is bringing their children until they open their presents Christmas morning.

109. Men think Thanksgiving dinner is just an elaborate pregame tailgate party.

110. Men do not follow rules because they insist that no one else does.

111. Men's mission statement is "If you don't know, fake it."

112. Men think they are right and the rest of the world should change.

113. Men do not understand why women make such a fuss about manners.

114. Men never notice when you get your hair cut.

115. Men think Valentine's Day is a scam cooked up by greeting-card companies.

116. Men think that if they told you they loved you back in 1987, it ought to be enough to last the rest of your life.

117. Men think cuddling is for wimps.

118. A man's best friend is his dog—and there's a reason for that.

119. Men will tell you they read *Playboy* for the articles.

120. Men will use a gas station bathroom the Board of Health wouldn't touch.

121. Men's favorite phrase is "I forgot."

122. Men shout encouraging words to their favorite team from the top row of a 56,000-seat stadium.

123. Men watch the Golf Channel, which consists of hours of whispering interrupted only by some guy named Jimbo demonstrating how you can make a chip shot from behind a tree using mirrors.

124. Men give pep talks to their 5-year-old's soccer team about being aggressive.

125. Men can conjugate curse words to fit any occasion.

126. When men are sick, they lie in bed and whine for as long as they can get away with it or until it is time to go to work—whichever comes first.

127. When you ask a man to do something, he says, "Make me a note."

128. Men will put a dish in the dishwasher with a pork chop still stuck to it.

129. Men do not consider salad to be real food.

130. Men think there is a shortcut to every destination.

131. Men don't believe you are really driving unless there is a clutch involved.

132. Men always drive full throttle and then slam on the brakes at the last minute.

133. Men get the shakes if you refold a map incorrectly.

134. Men don't use the following words: cute.

135. ... cozy.

136. ... precious.

137. ... tacky.

138. ... I was wrong ... My mistake ... I'm sorry ... or any similar phrases in any language whatsoever.

139. Men think anytime you disagree with them, it is your hormones talking.

140. Men think flowers are a waste of money.

141. Men think "Wanna see my tattoo?" is a good pickup line.

142. Men think Fabio is a wimp.

143. Men like to go places where you are encouraged to throw peanuts on the floor.

144. Men take "All You Can Eat" as a personal challenge.

145. Men call 2 pitchers of beer and an order of chicken wings at Hooters a business lunch.

146. Men think filets are for wimps.

147. Men never need anything—just ask them.

148. Men agree to go shopping with women and then spend the entire time glancing at their watches and looking as miserable as possible.

149. A man will ask his secretary to pick out something for his wife's birthday.

150. Men think sales are for wimps.

151. Men never want to "look like their mother dressed them."

152. Men wear whatever is clean ... or at least close to clean.

153. Men think mesh ball caps are an all-purpose accessory.

154. Men wear knickers to play golf and kilts to participate in the Highland Games, but they think having to wear a tie to their daughter's piano recital is a bit excessive.

155. For his wife's birthday, a man will splurge by taking her someplace where you do not have to carry your own tray.

156. Men do not care what the waiter's name is.

157. Men don't cut sandwiches.

158. Men think quiche is for wimps.

159. Men think bigger is always better: They buy Christmas trees the size of Giant Redwoods.

160. They order Grand Slam Breakfasts, Monster Burgers, and La La Palooza Sundaes.

161. Men buy riding mowers for 100-square-foot lawns.

162. When grilling, men build fires big enough to roast a dinosaur when there are only 4 hamburgers to cook.

163. Men buy big-screen TVs for 1-bedroom apartments.

164. When men go grocery shopping with women, they think that it is emasculating not to push the grocery cart.

165. Men taste grapes before they buy them.

166. Men laser-shop—they go straight to the one item they came for without looking to the right or the left, even if they are giving away Godiva samples.

167. Men think coupons are for wimps.

168. Men expect to have excuses made for them.

169. Men think "It's just business" covers just about everything.

170. Men speed-eat.

171. Men don't care what people think.

172. Men insist their sons carry on the family name even if it is Waldo Percival Outhouse III.

173. Men will be Lamaze coaches as long as they can have the ball game on in the labor room.

174. When men are in charge of the kids, they take them out for hamburgers and let them stay up until midnight.

175. Men cover their tracks with "Don't tell Mom."

176. A man lets his wife be the Wicked Witch of Discipline so he can be Uncle Fun.

177. Men goof around in church and get their kids in trouble.

178. When men take the kids to the store and come back with giant water cannons, they say, "They told me they needed them for school."

179. Men save the Super Detonator Water Cannon for themselves.

180. Men will subscribe to *Road and Track* even if they own a GEO.

181. Men buy Super Wax, bug and tar remover, chrome polish, and a rotary buffer and then take their car to the car wash.

182. Men put a cover on their car but send their kids out in the rain without a jacket.

183. Men still sigh when they think of their first car.

184. Men consider horn honking and the use of hand gestures central to the driving process.

185. Men make a game out of cutting people off in traffic.

186. Men will drive around ad infinitum looking for a parking spot right up front.

187. Men think valet parking is for wimps.

188. Men can live in a house for 25 years and not know where the vacuum cleaner is kept.

189. Men can watch 2 baseball games at once but can not find the jar of salsa in the refrigerator.

190. Men will help by washing the dishes and occasionally drying them but never putting them away because they do not know where they go.

191. If you ask men to help out with the laundry, they purposely put your sweaters in the dryer so you won't ask them again.

192. Men think a dinner party is successful if they have to loosen their belts before they leave the table.

193. When men are invited to a party, they say, "Let's go early so we can leave early."

194. Once at the party, men gravitate toward the TV set.

195. Men hover over the cheese dip.

196. Men adjust to weight gain by shifting their belts downward.

197. Men's pants shrink in the closet.

198. Men have lucky shirts.

199. Men's personal products all smell like trees.

200. Men know the offensive line coach of the Seattle Seahawks but not the name of their child's teacher.

201. Men deflect all serious decisions with "Go ask your mother."

202. Men try to skip over large portions of books when they read to their children.

203. Men never hear the kids get sick in the middle of the night.

204. Men won't look in the TV program guide—they much prefer to flip through all 144 channels.

205. Men think the Massage Recliner is the ultimate in living room furniture.

206. Men never use a simple hand tool when an electrical gadget can accomplish the same thing.

207. Men pretend they really understand woofers and tweeters.

208. Men buy gel, mousse, and extra-body hair spray for ¾ inch of hair.

209. Balding men comb their 7 remaining hairs in a swirl on top of their head.

210. Men play "Shirts and Skins" basketball years after "Shirts and Skins" would be much more pleasant to watch.

211. Men are going to start jogging ... tomorrow.

212. There is no worse fate for men than being henpecked—and they have invented several colorful phrases to describe that condition.

213. Every man thinks his job is harder than any woman's job.

214. Men believe that if they were not saddled with all their responsibilities, they'd be riding cross-country on a Harley.

215. Men hope the letters in *Penthouse* are true.

216. Men love: duct tape.

217. ... extension ladders.

218. ... anything that starts with the word "turbo."

219. ... attachments.

220. Men hate: costume parties.

221. ... panty hose hanging in the shower.

222. ... soap on a rope.

223. ... "fat-free" anything.

224. ... Julio Iglesias.

225. When you get right down to it, the only good thing about men is that they are not ... OTHER WOMEN!